Doohickey
and the **Robot**

JONATHAN EMMETT

Illustrated by Stephen Lewis

OXFORD
UNIVERSITY PRESS

Great Clarendon Street, Oxford OX2 6DP

Oxford University Press is a department of the University of Oxford.
It furthers the University's objective of excellence in research, scholarship,
and education by publishing worldwide in

Oxford New York

Auckland Bangkok Buenos Aires Cape Town Chennai
Dar es Salaam Delhi Hong Kong Istanbul Karachi Kolkata
Kuala Lumpur Madrid Melbourne Mexico City Mumbai Nairobi
São Paulo Shanghai Taipei Tokyo Toronto

Oxford is a registered trade mark of Oxford University Press
in the UK and in certain other countries

Database right Oxford University Press (maker)

First published 1999

10 9 8 7 6

ISBN 0 19 918687 1

Printed in Great Britain

Illustrations by Stephen Lewis
Photograph of Jonathan Emmett by Martin Emmett

If you want to find out more about Jonathan Emmett's books,
you can visit his web site at www.innotts.co.uk/-jonemmett/

Chapter One

Doohickey had just moved to a new town when he spotted a notice. It was stuck outside a big house at the end of his street.

Professor seeks young assistant to help with exciting experiments and interesting inventions.

Please ring the bell.

'That's the job for me,' said Doohickey. 'I need some more pocket-money.'

He pushed the doorbell. Then he jumped.

Weeeeyow-weeeeyow-weeeeyow! Kaaabooooom!

A loud alarm sounded inside the house, followed by a terrific explosion.

A window flew open at the top of the house. A cloud of thick smoke billowed out.

'What do you want?' coughed a voice from inside the cloud. 'Can't you see that I'm busy?'

The smoke cleared. The professor's
face peered down at Doohickey.

'Excuse me,' said Doohickey. 'My
name's Doohickey. I've come about the
job.'

'What job?' snapped the professor.

'As assistant,' said Doohickey. 'The
notice says you need one.'

'Oh, absolutely!' said the professor,
beginning to grin.

The notice had been up for over a year, but Doohickey was the first person to ask about it.

'Come on up!' said the professor. His head disappeared.

A moment later, the front door sprang half-open.

Doohickey peered inside. A huge mountain of post had stopped the door from opening properly. But there was no one there.

Doohickey felt sure that the door had opened for him, so he squeezed through into the hallway.

A buzzer sounded in Doohickey's ear. He was surprised to see a little air-ship bobbing in the hallway beside him.

Tiny propellers spun the ship around. Doohickey saw the words, 'FOLLOW ME' written in big red letters on its side.

Chapter Two

He followed the ship up a tall, winding staircase. He passed room after room stuffed full of strange-looking machines. Were they the professor's inventions?

Doohickey knew that he was supposed to go straight up the stairs, but he couldn't help himself. He popped into one of the rooms to take a closer look.

The first thing Doohickey came across was a computer screen fixed to a huge metal cage. The cage seemed to be stuffed full of straw.

Doohickey pushed his hand into it.

'Ouch!' he squealed, pulling it out again. A tiny needle was sticking out of his thumb.

There was a label fixed to the computer screen.

THE X-RAY-GRASSO-GRAPH
(for finding a needle in a haystack)

'Well, it didn't find this one,' said Doohickey crossly, as he stuck the needle back into the straw.

The next machine had lots of electric fans fixed beneath a large metal funnel. There was sand all over the floor. The label said:

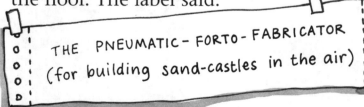

THE PNEUMATIC-FORTO-FABRICATOR
(for building sand-castles in the air)

'This looks like fun,' thought Doohickey. He switched it on.

Sand began trickling out of the funnel and the fans started spinning. Then the strangest thing happened.

The sand didn't fall on to the floor. It hung in the air. And slowly, it shaped itself into a floating castle.

Doohickey walked slowly around the machine. He couldn't believe what he was seeing.

Then all of a sudden, he bumped into someone else. When he saw who it was, he nearly jumped out of his skin.

The other person was him!

It was like looking in a mirror, except that there was no glass.

Doohickey reached out his hand and the other Doohickey did the same. Their fingers met in mid-air and he felt the warmth of his own hand pressing back. It was too creepy!

'Ughhh!' shivered Doohickey. He stepped backwards straight into the floating sand-castle.

The castle exploded and Doohickey
found himself in the middle of a
sandstorm. Sand blew everywhere, into
his eyes and up his nose.

Coughing and sneezing, he groped
his way back to the switch and turned
it off.

The sandstorm disappeared. And so
had the other Doohickey!

Then Doohickey noticed a large metal plate on the floor. There was another label on it.

THE STEREO-SELF DOUBLER
(for being in two places at once)

'Of course!' sighed Doohickey.

The metal plate was another of the professor's inventions. It had made the other Doohickey appear when he had stepped on to it.

I won't try that again, he thought. *It's a bit too spooky.*

A buzzer sounded. Doohickey saw the air-ship bobbing up and down in the doorway. It had come back to find him.

'I got lost,' said Doohickey. He couldn't think of a better excuse.

The ship buzzed again crossly and glided back towards the stairs.

'Coming,' said Doohickey.

Chapter Three

They reached the top of the house.

The air-ship led Doohickey into a smoky attic. It was stuffed full of books, test tubes and lumps of tangled wiring.

A small shaggy dog peered out
at him from beneath a workbench.
A cat lay sunning itself on the
window sill.

'What kept you?' asked the professor.
He was hunched over a heap of metal
in one corner.

'I was admiring some of your
inventions,' said Doohickey.

'Oh, those old things,' said the
professor. 'This,' he said, pointing to
the twisted heap of metal, 'is my latest
and greatest invention.'

'What is it?' asked Doohickey. It
didn't look very exciting. He expected
that it was a machine for getting blood
from a stone. Or for making omelettes
without breaking eggs.

'It's the RoBoffin 2000 Multi-Purpose
Robot,' said the professor, proudly.

'What does it do?' asked Doohickey.

'Absolutely anything!' said the
professor. 'Let me show you.'

The professor scribbled some words on to a scrap of paper. He fed the paper through the slot in the robot's chest.

Then he pressed a big button and stepped back.

The robot hummed and whirred for a bit. Then it climbed slowly to its feet. It was enormous. Its head almost scraped the attic ceiling.

The lights on the robot's face
flickered on and off. It looked as if it
was thinking about something.

And then … it painted a picture of the professor's dog.

It played a piece of music on the test tubes.

And it discovered three new ways of splitting the atom.

'Pretty good, eh?' said the professor, when the robot had finished.

'Cool!' said Doohickey. He was really amazed. The huge, heavy robot had whizzed around the attic, and it hadn't disturbed so much as a paper clip.

'It can do anything I ask it to,' said the professor.

'Anything?' asked Doohickey.

'Absolutely!' said the professor.

'Can I have a go?' asked Doohickey. He wanted to ask the robot to build a space rocket or tell him next week's winning lottery numbers.

'Absolutely not,' said the professor, 'it's far too complicated. Besides, I've got better things for you to do.'

'Such as?' said Doohickey. He was disappointed.

'Such as these,' said the professor, writing out a list. 'What month is it, by the way?'

'August,' said Doohickey.

'Summer! Already?' said the professor. He looked surprised. 'I must go out and pay my bills.'

He handed Doohickey the list of jobs.

'I'll be gone for the rest of the day,' he said, rushing out of the door. 'So these jobs should be finished by the time I get back. If you can't find anything, ask Newton.'

'Who's Newton?' shouted Doohickey, as the professor swept down the stairs.

'I am!' said the dog.

'You can talk!' said Doohickey, staring at the dog.

'How clever of you to notice,' said Newton.

'And the cat?' asked Doohickey, looking at the other animal. 'Can the cat talk too?'

'Of course not,' scoffed Newton, 'it's only a cat!'

Doohickey didn't know what to say to this. So he looked at the list of jobs the professor had given him.

Cook the dinner   Wash the dirty clothes

Hoover the hall carpet   Mow the lawn

Seal the leaky roof   Paint the front door

Water the pot plants   Walk th

Hang the picture   Feed the

'These jobs are all boring,' said Doohickey. 'The notice said I'd be helping with "exciting experiments and interesting inventions".'

'Of course it did,' said Newton, 'otherwise, you wouldn't have wanted the job.'

'Well, I don't want the job,' said Doohickey. 'I don't want to cook and clean all day.'

He tore up the list and threw it into
a bin.

'I'm off!' he said.

'Suit yourself,' said Newton.

Chapter Four

Doohickey went back down the winding staircase, past the rooms full of inventions.

Look at all these silly machines, he thought. Why doesn't the professor invent something useful; something that could do the housework?

Then he had a brain-wave. 'Of course!' he said. He set off upstairs again.

'Back so soon?' said Newton. 'I thought you didn't want the job.'

'I didn't,' said Doohickey, 'but I've had a brain-wave.'

'Oh, we get lots of them around here,' said the dog, yawning.

Doohickey picked the list out of the bin. He stuck it back together with some sticky tape.

'How does that look?' he asked, showing it to Newton.

Newton studied the list. 'It looks OK to me,' he said.

'Now for the clever bit,' said Doohickey.

He climbed on top of a stool and fed the stuck-together list through the slot in the robot's chest.

'Oh dear,' said Newton, shaking his head, 'the professor isn't going to like this.'

'The professor isn't going to find out!' said Doohickey. He hit the big button.

The robot hummed, whirred and then straightened itself up.

'It'll all end in tears,' sighed Newton.

The lights on the robot's face flickered on and off for a few minutes and then it stomped out of the attic.

'Piece of cake!' said Doohickey, grinning. 'Now, where can I take a nap?'

The robot stomped down the stairs
and into the professor's bathroom.

It grabbed a great armful of dirty
clothes. Then it carried them down to
the kitchen. But instead of putting
them into the washing machine it
stuffed them into the oven.

Next, it took some meat and
vegetables out of the fridge. It chopped
and sliced them to make a delicious
stew. Then it emptied the whole lot
into the washing machine!

After that, it brought the lawnmower into the house and ran it over the hall carpet.

And it took the Hoover outside and sucked the leaves off the lawn.

Chapter Five

The professor's neighbours were used
to strange things going on at his
house. But they had never seen
anything quite like the robot.

'What do you think it's up to?' asked
one of them. The robot had just
fetched a hammer and nails. It was
now nailing up the front door.

'Perhaps the professor's gone away,' suggested another, 'and he's afraid that someone will try and break in.'

The robot didn't seem to mind that everyone was looking at it. It propped a ladder up against the side of the house.

Then it climbed to the top and began to brush bright green paint all over the roof.

Newton was half asleep when the
robot stomped into the attic carrying
a watering can.

'The pot plants are in the living
room,' said the dog, helpfully.
The huge machine lumbered
towards him.

'I should have known something would go wrong!' he sighed, as the robot emptied the watering can over his head.

Doohickey was still fast asleep on the professor's bed.

'Wake up! Wake up!' barked Newton, shaking his wet fur in the boy's face.

'What's wrong?' yawned Doohickey, rubbing his eyes.

'Oh, just about everything!' said
Newton.

'What's happened?' asked
Doohickey.

'The robot's gone mad,' said
Newton. 'Last time I saw it, it was
pulling up the pot plants. I told you
it would all end in tears.'

Chapter Six

They ran downstairs to the hall. The carpet was covered in shredded paper.

'What's happened here?' asked Doohickey. He looked dazed.

Newton held up a scrap of paper with a postage stamp stuck to it.

'It's the professor's letters,' he said.

'But it looks like they've been through a shredder!' said Doohickey.

'Or a lawnmower …' suggested Newton.

In the kitchen they found the dirty clothes burning in the oven and the stew churning around inside the washing machine.

'I don't understand,' groaned Doohickey. 'What went wrong?'

'The robot seems to have got the jobs mixed up,' said Newton.

'But how?' said Doohickey. 'You saw the list that I gave it. You said it was OK!'

'I said it looked OK,' said Newton, 'but I didn't read it.'

'Why not?' wailed Doohickey.

The dog looked uncomfortable.

'You *can* read, can't you?' asked Doohickey.

'Of course not,' said Newton, 'I'm only a dog.'

Just then the robot stomped in through the back door. It was trailing a bunch of bedraggled pot plants behind it – having taken the plants for a walk.

The robot dragged the plants through to the living room and dropped them back into their pots.

'Stop at once!' commanded Doohickey, standing in front of it.

But the robot barged straight past him, into the kitchen.

'It won't stop until it's done everything on the list,' explained Newton.

'So what's it doing now?' asked Doohickey.

The robot ripped the fridge away from the wall and carried it upstairs.

'Beats me,' said Newton.

The robot carried the fridge all the way up to the attic. It stopped in front of Newton's freshly painted picture.

It opened the fridge door, took out a piece of pie, and jammed it into the mouth painted on the picture of Newton.

It made a hole in the picture and the pie fell out of the other side. The robot took some more food and stuffed it into the hole.

'It's feeding the picture,' said Newton.

'But it's supposed to hang the picture ...' said Doohickey, trying to remember the professor's list.

'... and feed the cat?' finished Newton.

'So that means that ... next ... it will try to ... *oh, no!*' wailed Doohickey, as the robot set off towards the sleeping cat.

Chapter Seven

The professor knew that there was something wrong when he saw the crowd of people standing outside his house.

He knew that something was *terribly* wrong when he saw the green paint dripping from his roof, and heard the cat screeching in the attic.

He bounded up to the front door and ... found that it was nailed shut.

He rushed around the back of the house and in the back door. He could smell something burning, but he didn't stop to find out what.

He ran straight up the stairs, three steps at a time, and burst into the attic.

The attic was a nightmare.

The robot was lurching around the room with a length of electric cable. It was trying to catch the cat.

Luckily, the terrified cat was staying one leap ahead of it.

Between the two of them, they had managed to knock over most of the professor's equipment.

Doohickey was jumping up and
down in front of the robot, trying to
hit the buttons on its chest.

Newton was sitting on a tall
cupboard, enjoying the show.

Without saying a word, the professor strode across the room and hit the big button on the robot's chest.

The robot stopped chasing the cat, let out a little sigh and toppled over. A scrap of paper rolled out of the slot in its chest.

The professor snatched up the paper and looked at it.

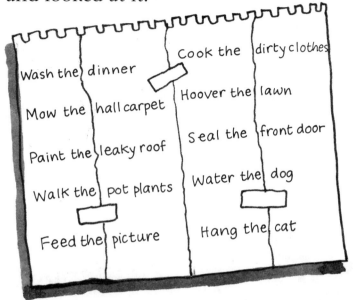

'Who is responsible for this?' he said, quietly,

'Don't look at me,' said Newton, 'I'm only a dog.'

'Doohickey!' said the professor.

'Erm ... I was ... just err ...' panted Doohickey.

The professor gave Doohickey a hard stare.

'You see … I just, um … thought that …' Doohickey tried to explain.

The professor gave Doohickey an even harder stare.

'It was all my fault,' said Doohickey.

'Absolutely,' agreed the professor.

Doohickey gazed around the attic. It had been untidy to start with. But that was nothing to how it looked now.

The professor was giving him another hard stare.

'Oh,' said Doohickey slowly, 'I suppose you want me to clear up all this mess?'

'Absolutely,' repeated the professor.

'Righto,' said Doohickey, 'I'd better get on with it.' It would take hours to tidy up on his own.

He looked around for Newton, but the dog had vanished.

'Um, I don't suppose,' he said, carefully, looking at the professor, 'I could use the robot to …?'

'*Absolutely not!*' shouted the professor.

About the author

The idea for this book came to me while I was typing another story. I was supposed to type 'mow the lawn and hoover the carpet', but I got it mixed up and typed  'mow the carpet' by mistake. I thought how funny it would be if other jobs got mixed up and how that might happen.

My favourite character is Newton. He is quite happy to let other people think he is cleverer than he really is.

Other Treetops books at this level include:
Dads Win Prizes by Debbie White
Scrapman and Scrapcat by Carolyn Bear
Me and My Newt by Pippa Goodhart
A Kitten in Daisy Street by Pat Belford
Kid Wonder and the Terrible Truth by Stephen Elboz

Also available in packs
Stage 12+ pack D   0 19 918688 X
Stage 12+ class pack D   0 19 918689 8